CHRISTINE McCVIE

Songbird's Flight

WRITTEN BY:
MIRA CHERYL

© **Mira Cheryl, 2024.**

All rights reserved. No part of this publication may be reproduced, stored in a retrieval system, or transmitted in any form or by any means, electronic, mechanical, photocopying, recording, or otherwise, without the prior written permission of the publisher, except for the inclusion of brief quotations in critical reviews and certain noncommercial uses permitted by copyright law.

DISCLAIMER

This book is intended as a brief and engaging biography, designed for fans to enjoy a glimpse into the life and career of **Christine MCcvie**. While every effort has been made to ensure the accuracy of the information presented, **it is not intended to be a comprehensive or definitive account**. Please enjoy this book as a tribute to a remarkable actress and singer.

Please note that all trademarks and copyrights mentioned within this book belong to their respective owners and are used in this book for informational purposes only.

TABLE OF CONTENTS

TABLE OF CONTENTS..2

INTRODUCTION..3

EARLY LIFE.. 5

FINDING HER PLACE...9

SONGWRITING POWERHOUSE...21

FLEETWOOD MAC..27

A TRIUMPHANT RETURN...42

BEYOND FLEETWOOD MAC..46

INTRODUCTION

Born Christine Perfect in the little village of Bouth, Lancashire, on July 12, 1943, Christine Anne McVie was more than just a pianist. She was a storyteller with a voice that could calm and soar, a weaver of songs. Her path, which entwined with the iconic band Fleetwood Mac, created a tapestry of musical genius that still enthrals listeners all around, marked by both personal successes and sorrows. The music industry sadly lost this legendary singer-songwriter and keyboardist on November 30, 2022, but her legacy will forever remain etched in the annals of rock and pop history.

Over her career, McVie has received recognition for her contributions to music. In 1998, McVie and her Fleetwood Mac comrades secured their place in musical history with their induction into the Rock and Roll Hall of Fame. The same year, they received the Brit Award for Outstanding Contribution to Music, demonstrating their ongoing influence on British music. Recognizing her pioneering attitude and impact on next generations of musicians, McVie also earned individual honours like the Trailblazer Award at the UK Americana Awards in 2021 and the coveted Ivor Novello Award for Lifetime Achievement in 2014.

Christine McVie's legacy weaves the fabric of musical history. Audiences of all ages still find resonance in her songs because of their classic melodies and moving words. Her warm and expressive voice is still a comfort and motivation tool. And her keyboard playing, a fundamental component of Fleetwood Mac's trademark sound, still captivates listeners all over. Although the songbird has departed, her music will continue to resonate in our hearts, ensuring her legacy endures for future generations.

EARLY LIFE

The tale of Christine Anne Perfect starts in the peaceful village of Greenodd, tucked away in the Furness district of Lancashire, England, not among the glitter of a huge city. Her musical future first took root in the Bearwood neighbourhood of Smethwick, near Birmingham, where she was born on July 12, 1943.

Her family wove music into their fabric. Concert violinist and respected music lecturer Cyril Percy Absell Perfect, her father, taught at St. Peter's College of Education in Birmingham. Teaching violin at St Philip's Grammar School allowed him to share his love of music with others. Working as a medium, psychic, and faith healer, Christine's mother, Beatrice Edith Maud (née Reece), had a special relationship with the spiritual world. Her grandpa was a renowned organist at Westminster Abbey, therefore augmenting this rich tapestry of cultural legacy.

Living in this setting, Christine's musical path started at the young age of four when she first came upon the piano. Her first taste of music was fleeting, but owing to the support of a local musician and brother John's friend, her enthusiasm rekindled. This time the spark started a fire. She focused assiduously on classical instruction until the age of fifteen, sharpening her abilities and laying a basis that would be valuable in years to come.

But Christine's growing musical vitality couldn't fit the regimented universe of classical music. Particularly the songs of Fats Domino, the rebellious energy of rock and roll caught her imagination and pointed her in a different direction. Her brother John, in recognition of her ability and dedication, gave her a Fats Domino songbook, further stoking her love of this fascinating new sound. Her musical career also grew, much influenced by the Everly Brothers' catchy songs and close harmonies.

While studying her love of sculpting at the Moseley School of Art in Birmingham, Christine found herself drawn to the energetic blues culture sweeping across Britain, with the hope of becoming an art teacher. This period, typified by a rebirth of interest in American blues music, gave new artists plenty of space to investigate and test ideas. She first got to know two artists who would be crucial in her early career: Stan Webb and Andy Silvester.

Understanding Christine's natural musical ability, Webb and Silvester asked her to play with their band, Sounds of Blue. She jumped at the chance to lend her unique vocals and piano abilities to their bluesy vibe. Before Spencer Davis, a rising star in the British music industry, started the Spencer Davis Group with Steve Winwood, she had the opportunity to share the stage with him.

Christine briefly travelled to London following her art college graduation, working as a department shop window dresser. Still, her heart remained firmly in music. She excitedly rejoined her former colleagues when she found that Silvester and Webb were starting a new blues band called Chicken Shack, this time serving as their pianist, keyboardist, and backup vocalist.

Chicken Shack gave Christine a stage on which to grow her musical personality and exhibit her skill. Christine wrote and sung their first hit, "It's Okay with Me Baby," with soulfulness. She participated on two studio albums with the band, her Sonny Thompson-style piano playing and emotionally driven vocals clearly displaying her real blues sensibilities.

Covering Ellington Jordan's "I'd Rather Go Blind," a song highlighting Christine's strong lead vocals and garnering her great popularity, Chicken Shack's breakthrough came. Melody Maker recognized her vocal prowess by naming her the UK's top female vocalist for 1969 and 1970.

Meanwhile, Christine's personal life was also undergoing significant changes. She married Fleetwood Mac bassist John McVie in 1968. She left the band in 1969, caught between her growing success with Chicken Shack and her need to be with her spouse. This signalled the end of one chapter and the beginning of another as she got ready to travel on a fresh musical adventure with Fleetwood Mac, one that would define her legacy and confirm her position among the most lasting legends in music.

FINDING HER PLACE

Christine McVie originally became familiar with Fleetwood Mac from a fan standpoint. Their paths often crossed those of the developing blues-rock band while she was with Chicken Shack. McVie's first business link with Fleetwood Mac came from both groups signing under the same Blue Horizon label. She offered her piano skills as a session musician on Peter Green's second studio album, Mr. Wonderful, released in 1968. This early gathering prepared the ground for a musical collaboration blossoming in the future years.

Driven by her growing reputation and clear talent, McVie debuted Christine Perfect, her first solo album, in 1970. Originally titled "I'm on My Way," as hinted during the early single releases, the album ultimately retained Perfect's birth name, possibly as a subconscious acknowledgement of the distinct artistic identity she was developing. The album cover, featuring a reflective perfection within a soft-focus dreamscape, further emphasises this concept of self-discovery.

Reflecting the several influences guiding her early skill, "Christine Perfect" is an interesting blend of musical styles. Her beautiful voice, reminiscent of old blues and soul singers, flows naturally over a tapestry of blues-infused rock, folk-inspired ballads, and hints of emerging pop sensibilities. Including a combination of original compositions and well-chosen covers, the CD showcases her adaptability as a songwriter and interpreter.

Perfect's own band provides a rich background for her passionate singing and piano playing: Top Topham and Rick Hayward on guitars, Martin Dunsford on bass, and Chris Harding on drums. They are a close-knit ensemble. Their lively and simple interaction creates a rich sound environment that highlights Perfect's emotive delivery. Including "When You Say," a song featuring future Fleetwood Mac colleagues Danny Kirwan and John McVie, adds an interesting dimension to the record. Covering Kirwan's piece from Fleetwood Mac's "Then Play On" album, this collaboration anticipates the musical synergy she will soon define her career with.

Perfect delivered arguably the most remarkable rendition of Etta James' soul classic "I'd Rather Go Blind" on the CD. Originally a smash for Chicken Shack with Perfect on lead vocals, this powerful ballad emphasises the raw feeling and vocal ability that would define her ultimately. Her solo album features the Chicken Shack variation, which serves as an intriguing connection between her past and future creative personas, given that both musicians were associated with Blue Horizon recordings.

Reissued under numerous titles in the years following its release, "Christine Perfect" highlighted McVie's growing relevance in her broad repertory. It resurfaced in 1976 under the name "The Legendary Christine Perfect Album," alluding to her rising profile with Fleetwood Mac. 2008 saw the release of a more all-encompassing edition, "Christine Perfect: The Complete Blue Horizon Sessions," which contained bonus tracks and outtakes stressing her creative process. Fascinatingly, despite its claim to completeness, this version omits "I'd Rather Go Blind," perhaps in reaction to licensing issues or a desire to differentiate it from Chicken Shack recordings.

Reflecting on her solo debut, McVie expressed nostalgia and self-criticism. Though she recognized the album's significance in launching her career, she admitted to feeling some guilt over some of the tracks, believing several lacked the creative maturity she eventually achieved with Fleetwood Mac. She explained this away as extraneous pressures and uncertainty about her musical direction at the moment. She felt she truly came into her own as an artist only once she moved into Fleetwood Mac's cooperative environment.

"Christine Perfect" is an amazing and essential component of McVie's musical puzzle even now. Her latter reflections notwithstanding. Capturing her raw ability, shifting artistry, and numerous inspirations that shaped her unique voice, it offers a rare view into the early years of a musical legend. The record showcases the journey of self-discovery that preceded her ascent to fame, a path that ultimately shaped her into the renowned Christine McVie, the essence of Fleetwood Mac.

Fleetwood Mac was experiencing concurrent personal change. Peter Green, the band's founder and principal inspiration, created a hole that proved difficult to fill in 1970. Seeking another musical direction, the band fought to maintain momentum. They encouraged McVie, who already loved their work, to contribute as a keyboardist, thereby bringing her own sound and composition skills.

Before officially joining, McVie had already offered piano and backup vocals—unacknowledged—for their 1970 record Kiln House. She even demonstrated artistic adaptability in designing the CD's striking cover. Knowing the band's music and being able to fit their sound made her an ideal addition. McVie announced a shift for Fleetwood Mac. Her arrival brought the band—which had been dangerously near to breaking apart—new stability and direction. Mick Fleetwood, the band's drummer and namesake, later remarked, "Christine became the glue [that held the band together]." She finished our sound very brilliantly.

Fleetwood Mac was at a crossroads negotiating a period of change and reinvention in the summer of 1971. The band was keen to investigate fresh sound environments because founding member Peter Green had left a void last year. Their fifth studio album, "Future Games," which came out on September 3rd, marked a major turning point, a break from their blues-rock beginnings, and a daring move toward a more melodic, pop-infused sound. Two important additions to the Fleetwood Mac family—Christine McVie as a full-fledged member and the entrance of American guitarist Bob Welch, whose musical influences would significantly affect the band's future direction—served to further drive this aural change.

"Future Games" began with the "Kiln House" sessions in 1970. Seeking stability and fresh inspiration, the band asked Christine Perfect, wife of bassist John McVie, to add her piano skills and songwriting aptitude when Green left. Perfect, a gifted musician in her own right, quickly became indispensable with her soulful vocals and unique piano playing that complemented the band's evolving sound. Her significant contributions led to her swift acceptance as a full member, the adoption of the name Christine McVie, and the beginning of a musical journey that would forever intertwine her destiny with Fleetwood Mac.

But another unanticipated development occurred just as the band started a tour to support "Kiln House." Known for his flamboyant stage appearance and love of classic rock and roll, guitarist and vocalist Jeremy Spencer abruptly departed the band to join the contentious religious organisation, the Children of God, in February 1971. The band's lineup suffered greatly from this unexpected absence, which also prompted a frantic search for a substitute.

Now enter Bob Welch, an American musician with a varied musical history anchored on R&B, jazz, and pop. Welch's entrance gave Fleetwood Mac's sound a new vitality and dimension. His melodic sensitivities and taste for complex harmonies matched the band's changing direction, driving them farther from their blues roots and toward a more polished, pop-oriented approach.

Recording "Future Games" took place against the backdrop of artistic inquiry and a sense of just-acquired independence. The London Advision Studios sessions also encountered challenges. Christine McVie remembered the challenges they faced recording "Sands of Time," a sophisticated piece requiring exacting attention to detail and careful musician interaction. Notwithstanding the challenges, the band persisted. Their common vision and combined will helped them to distil the core of their changing sound.

A great story about the album's production centres on the last song, "What a Shame." After finishing the first song, the band sent the album to their record label, only to face an unexpected demand: the label insisted on an eighth song to complete the tracklist. Given this ultimatum, the band composed "What a Shame," a bluesy, improvised tune that met the label's criteria and reflected their unvarnished vitality. Born out of need, this last-minute addition finally gave the album a raw, unvarnished quality and highlighted the band's improvisational prowess and ability to create magic in the moment.

Despite peaking at a meagre 91 on the US Billboard 200 list, "Future Games" gained enduring popularity when the RIAA certified it gold in 2000. Still, the album's importance goes beyond mere monetary success. It marks a turning point in Fleetwood Mac's development, a daring step toward a new musical identity marked by melodic songwriting, varied inspirations, and growing importance of Christine McVie's contributions. It was a glimpse into a future packed with possibilities—a future that would eventually propel them to unprecedented heights of success and cement their reputation as one of the most legendary bands in music history.

Fleetwood Mac's "Bare Trees," their sixth studio album and a moving meditation on a band negotiating a period of significant transition, debuted in March 1972. Though it would be the last album to feature guitarist Danny Kirwan, whose creative contributions shone brilliantly despite the approaching uncertainty, it also provided a stage for Christine McVie to really blossom as a songwriter and vocalist, her unique voice adding warmth and emotional depth to the album's tapestry.

Notwithstanding the underlying conflicts and doubts, "Bare Trees" is evidence of the band's tenacity and their capacity to turn their emotional terrain into song. The title of the album, which suggests a clear winter picture, aptly expresses the reflective and sad attitude that permeates several of the songs. In later analysis of the record, Mick Fleetwood praised Danny Kirwan's "chops with layering techniques and the ability to know what's right and wrong in the studio."

On "Bare Trees," nevertheless, Christine McVie's vocal clarity and composition really shine. Her contributions give the auditory environment of the record warmth, emotional depth, and a clearly feminine viewpoint. The moving ballad "Homeward Bound" catches the fatigue and yearning for home that may accompany a life on the road. Later on, Fleetwood said, McVie's beautiful singing and poignant words really spoke to a profound yearning for "a proper night's rest in her own bed."

Another McVie treasure, "Spare Me a Little of Your Love," is a deep cry for connection and understanding that highlights McVie's ability to create emotionally relevant songs that appeal to all human experience. Her voice, imbued with both vulnerability and strength, soars over a delicate arrangement of piano, acoustic guitar, and subdued strings to create a mesmerising environment of intimacy and emotional honesty.

McVie's musical contributions balance emotional depth and the CD, therefore providing a vital counterweight to Kirwan's more introspective and occasionally stormy compositions. Her presence as a vocalist and songwriter is crucial to the whole fabric of "Bare Trees," highlighting her developing confidence and her capacity to create songs with universal and personal themes that appeal to both. While "Bare Trees" signified the end of an era for Fleetwood Mac with Kirwan's departure, it also indicated the beginning of a new chapter, one in which Christine McVie's contributions would become increasingly significant.

"Penguin," Fleetwood Mac's seventh studio album, debuted in March 1973 as evidence of their ongoing development and fortitude. This album caught the band negotiating yet another phase of change, a vivid mix of bluesy grit, melodic rock, and soulful inquiry. Christine McVie stayed a constant presence even as guitarist Danny Kirwan left and welcomed new members Bob Weston and Dave Walker; her songs and unique vocals provide a vital anchor among the changing waves.

"Penguin" sprang from the wreckage of transformation. The absence of Kirwan, following a fight with band members during the "Bare Trees" tour, left the band's dynamic lacking. Seeking to close this void and venture into uncharted sonic territory, Fleetwood Mac hired vocalist Dave Walker, previously of Savoy Brown and The Idle Race, and guitarist Bob Weston, known for his slide guitar ability and past work with Long John Baldry. While Weston's guitar expertise gave the band's musical palette a fresh dimension, Walker's arrival injected a raw, bluesy energy into their sound.

But Christine McVie's keyboard work and songwriting provide a vital thread of consistency amid this period of change. Her contributions on "Penguin" highlighted her adaptability and developing confidence as a songwriter, deftly fusing the band's developing sound with her own melodic sensibilities. Songs like "Remember Me" and "Dissatisfied" show her ability to create emotionally powerful songs and deliver them with her unique soulful expression and warmth.

Notable, too, is McVie's piano performance on "Penguin," which gives the auditory terrain of the record texture and depth. Her unique keyboard technique, sometimes distinguished by its subdued elegance and bluesy inflections, accentuates the band's dynamic interaction to produce a rich and complex musical tapestry. Her piano offers a gentle counterpoint to Weston's slide guitar on songs like "Night Watch," therefore producing an entrancing interaction of light and shadow.

Fascinatingly, the "Penguin" recording broke with the conventional studio environment. The band chose a more personal and laid-back environment rather than a London studio, hence bringing the Rolling Stones Mobile Studio to their shared house, Benifold, Hampshire. Christine McVie's unusual suggestion was to create a more creative and natural atmosphere, therefore enabling the band to record a more natural and real sound.

Although "Penguin" had little economic success—it ranked Top 50 in the US charts—Dave Walker's incorporation proved to be fleeting. It became clear on the next tour and during the making of their second album, "Mystery to Me," that Walker's vocals and approach did not entirely fit the band's changing direction. Walker amiably split from Fleetwood Mac by June 1973, leaving a brief but unforgettable impression on their musical path.

SONGWRITING POWERHOUSE

Fleetwood Mac released their eighth studio album, "Mystery to Me," in October 1973, marking a pivotal moment for the band. With guitarist Bob Weston's departure and their last album produced in England for some years, it symbolised the end of an era and highlighted Christine McVie's developing compositional ability and vocal impact. This album is evidence of Fleetwood Mac's ongoing tenacity, their ability to negotiate internal strife and lineup changes while still creating mesmerising music that deftly combined their blues-rock roots with a growing pop sensibility.

The making of "Mystery to Me" was surrounded by doubt and change. Still recovering from Danny Kirwan's death and getting used to Bob Weston and Dave Walker, the band found itself at a turning point. Walker's leaving the recording sessions accentuated the flux and instability even further. Notwithstanding these obstacles, the key members—Mick Fleetwood, John McVie, Christine McVie, and Bob Welch—persevered, directing their creative energy into an album that reflected their changing musical vision.

Christine McVie's efforts on "Mystery to Me" were absolutely transformative, highlighting her development as a performer and songwriter. Her songs gave the album's sonic tapestry a rich layer of warmth and emotional depth when combined with her characteristic mix of soulful voice, melodic piano playing, and honest words. Tracks like "Just Crazy Love," a bluesy, soulful number brimming with raw emotion, and "Why," a poignant ballad delving into the intricacies of love and loss, showcase her adaptability and her capacity to craft songs that resonate with vulnerability and strength.

McVie had an impact beyond her own works. Her unique vocals for Bob Welch's "Keep On Going," a monument to her adaptability and the cooperative attitude that pervaded the band's creative process, also add character. Understanding McVie's voice's special tone and emotional resonance, Welch thought her performance would more faithfully capture the spirit of the song. A trademark of Fleetwood Mac's creative energy, this cooperative approach highlighted their capacity to combine their abilities and produce music that went beyond individual efforts.

Recording "Mystery to Me" carried on the band's investigation of unusual studio environments. Like with "Penguin," they decided to transport the Rolling Stones Mobile Studio—which they had visited—to their shared residence, Benifold, Hampshire. Promoted by Christine

McVie, this strategy sought to create a more laid-back and creative environment so the band may record a more natural and organic sound. In a 2003 interview, Mick Fleetwood considered the benefits of this strategy, stressing its affordability and the band flexibility it allowed.

Still, the "Mystery to Me" era was not without challenges. Tensions grew during the band's 1973 American tour. When it came to light, Bob Weston was seeing Jenny, Mick Fleetwood's wife. The band suffered a great divide from this personal betrayal, which finally resulted in Weston's firing. The tour was suddenly called off, and the band went back to England to face Clifford Davis, their manager, who, in a dubious action, sent another set of musicians on the road under Fleetwood Mac, claiming ownership of the name.

"Mystery to Me" attained modest financial success in spite of this inner strife and outside pressure. It peaked at number 67 on the US Billboard 200 list and finally received a gold certification from the RIAA. Still, the album's importance goes beyond mere chart accomplishment. Showcasing their tenacity, openness to experimentation, and the growing impact of Christine McVie's talent, it marks a turning point in Fleetwood Mac's development.

Fleetwood Mac's eighth studio album, "Heroes Are Hard to Find," debuted in September 1974 and caught the band negotiating a turbulent period of inner strife and outside pressure. Last to feature Bob Welch before his departure, this record marked a major change for the band both geographically and artistically. Driven by a want for a fresh start and a better relationship with their record label, it was their first studio album recorded in the United States. Christine McVie's vocals and composition stood brilliantly among the chaos, offering a feeling of consistency and continuity as the band headed forward.

The composition of "Heroes Are Hard to Find" was overshadowed by a series of obstacles that threatened to derail the band entirely. The fallout from Bob Weston's affair with Mick Fleetwood's wife had created a deep rift, leading to a temporary disbandment and a legal battle with their manager, Clifford Davis, who attempted to capitalise on the situation by assembling a completely new lineup and touring under the Fleetwood Mac name. This ambitious move pushed the band to fight for their very identity, a struggle that would ultimately lead them to migrate to Los Angeles and chart a new route.

Christine McVie, first concerned about the transfer to America, finally embraced the opportunity for a fresh start. Her vital contributions to "Heroes Are Hard to Find" gave the work consistency and continuity throughout the tumult. As always, her songwriting was distinguished by its emotional candour, melodic richness, and perceptive words. Highlights of her flexibility and ability to deftly mix several genres were "Bad Loser," a bluesy rocker with a powerful rhythm, and "Come a Little Bit Closer," a delicate ballad highlighting her softer side.

McVie's equally remarkable keyboard work on the record gives the band's sound character and depth. Often marked by its subdued elegance and bluesy inflections, her piano playing offered a wonderful counterpoint to Welch's guitar performance, effectively driving the songs ahead. Her piano creates a delicate basis for songs like "She's Changing Me," where Welch's vocals soar; on "Angel," her keyboard work adds some sorrow to the song's introspective atmosphere.

Though there was no major single, "Heroes Are Hard to Find" had modest commercial success, landing at number 34 on the Billboard 200 chart—a noteworthy accomplishment for the band at the time. The title song of the album, a moving meditation on the difficulties of establishing lasting relationships in an environment undergoing change, connected with fans and caught the band's own efforts to negotiate a trying moment.

Still, the influence of the album goes beyond mere chart success. It marks a turning point in Fleetwood Mac's development and evidence of their fortitude and capacity to conquer difficulty. The success of the record owed much to Christine McVie's skills as a vocalist and lyricist, which gave a feeling of consistency and continuity among the upheaval. Her presence, together with Mick Fleetwood's and John McVie's relentless dedication, guaranteed that Fleetwood Mac would survive the storm and come out stronger, ready to welcome the next phase of their extraordinary trip.

FLEETWOOD MAC

With the release of their tenth studio album, self-titled and usually affectionately referred to as the "White Album" by their loyal fans, July 1975 saw a dramatic change in Fleetwood Mac's path. This record suggested a rebirth, a shedding of old skin, and an embrace of a new era bursting with creative energy and commercial success. Although Bob Welch, a key player in the band's post-Peter Green years, was leaving, it also heralded the arrival of the dynamic pair, Lindsey Buckingham and Stevie Nicks, who gave Fleetwood Mac a fresh, distinctly Californian sound. Christine McVie, the band's constant anchor, not only adjusted but flourished amid this metamorphosis; her vocals and songwriting were crucial in determining this new direction.

During a visit to Sound City Studios with producer Keith Olsen, Mick Fleetwood coincidentally discovered a demo tape by the relatively unknown duo, Buckingham Nicks. Particularly the captivating solo on the song "Frozen Love immediately struck Fleetwood; Lindsey Buckingham's superb guitar work really hit home. Seeing a similar spirit and a possible change agent, Fleetwood quickly invited Buckingham to join Fleetwood Mac. One non-negotiable, though, was that Stevie Nicks, his musical and romantic partner, had to be part of the agreement. Despite their unpredictable relationship, Buckingham and Nicks' creative impulses were inseparable. Sensing their unquestionable talent and magic potential, Fleetwood agreed to bring them both on board.

This fateful choice would prove to be a pivotal moment for Fleetwood Mac. Arriving with a distinctive mix of folk-rock sensibilities and a West Coast attitude that gave the band new vitality, Buckingham and Nicks brought something different. Their arrival set off a creative flame that resulted in a period of outstanding musical inquiry and teamwork.

Ever the flexible and encouraging band member, Christine McVie embraced this new era with wide arms. She embraced Buckingham's production ideas since she saw his ability to shape and polish her musical vision. Their working relationship turned out to be successful, Buckingham's sharp ear for production and arrangement accentuating McVie's already great songwriting. Buckingham said in a later interview, "It was so clear right away that Christine and I had this thing," noting McVie's openness to his opinions. She was merely looking for guidance. She was willing for me to play with her music.

On this self-titled album, McVie's songwriting kept improving, proving her adaptability and remarkable ability to create emotionally strong songs that really connected with audiences. Reaching the Top 20 in the US charts, "Over My Head," a mournful ballad examining the complexity of love and longing, became the album's breakthrough single. Her other works, including "Say You Love Me," an exhilarating pop-rock gem that soared the charts, "Warm Ways," a profound expression of compassion and warmth, and "Sugar Daddy," further cemented her reputation as a formidable songwriter. She also collaborated with Buckingham on "World Turning," demonstrating her ability to work seamlessly with her new bandmates.

"Fleetwood Mac" became a spectacular commercial success, reaching the top of the US Billboard 200 chart and achieving multi-platinum status. It produced three Top 20 songs and signalled the start of the band's hitherto unheard-of run of popularity. The album's ongoing appeal is a testament to the creative synergy of its members, the depth of their music, and their ability to build a strong emotional connection with fans. Christine McVie, a constant throughout the band's various transitions, played a vital role in its triumph, her songwriting and vocal talents providing a crucial thread of continuity and emotional depth. "Fleetwood Mac" marked a fresh start, a rebirth that would propel the band toward superstardom and confirm their rank among the most legendary bands in music history.

Fleetwood Mac's fame grew, and so did the complexity and entwining of their personal lives. Amidst the frenzy of touring and recording in 1976, McVie started an affair with the band's lighting director. This rocky relationship led her to create "You Make Loving Fun," a heartfelt and genuine declaration of love and desire that became a Top 10 hit on their following album, "Rumors.

1976 saw Fleetwood Mac riding a tide of popularity after their self-titled ninth album's release. Underneath their apparent glory, though, a tempest of personal struggle was building. Divorce, breakups, and adultery were casting a shadow over the band's creative efforts as their internal relationships broke apart. Still, among this emotional tempest, they started working on "Rumours," an album that would rank among the most famous and enduring records in music history. The band's steady anchor, Christine McVie, gracefully and resiliently negotiated this storm, her lyrics and vocals helping to define the emotional terrain and long legacy of the record.

30

The band battled internally from several angles. After eight years of marriage, John and Christine McVie chose to divorce. Their personal relationship was breaking under the weight of celebrity and ongoing travel demands. Once inseparable, the pair now only discussed musical concerns, permanently damaging their personal relationship. Creative sparks drove Lindsey Buckingham and Stevie Nicks, the band's recently minted star team, into a turbulent on-again, off-again relationship, disrupted by explosive conflict. Even the band's dynamic drummer, Mick Fleetwood, struggled personally after learning of his wife Jenny's infidelity with a close friend.

The media, eager to capitalise on the band's personal tragedies, occasionally sensationalised and distorted the turbulence. For example, Buckingham and Nicks were wrongly identified as the parents of Fleetwood's daughter Lucy after being pictured with her, while Christine McVie was incorrectly believed to be hospitalised with a major illness. These invasions of their personal life added yet another level of stress to an already explosive scenario.

Band members continued their artistic efforts despite the emotional turbulence. Early 1976 saw them starting to create fresh work in Florida, their personal conflicts boiling under the surface. Creative conflicts drove

Fleetwood and John McVie to decide to split from their producer, Keith Olsen, during these sessions. Olsen's method, they felt, did not sufficiently highlight the rhythm section—a fundamental component of Fleetwood Mac's sound. This choice revealed their increasing confidence and their will to take more charge of their artistic direction.

The band began recording "Rumours" at the Record Plant in Sausalito, California, in February 1976. Together with engineers Ken Caillat and Richard Dashut, the band divided production responsibilities to create a cooperative atmosphere encouraging experimentation and creativity. However, the studio itself, a large, windowless wooden structure, proved to be problematic. Many band members complained about the austere surroundings and yearned to record in the convenience of their own houses. But Fleetwood stayed strong, adamant that they stay at the Record Plant.

The band members channelled their inner turbulence into their songs despite less-than-perfect settings. Studio sessions turned into a unique blend of artistic brilliance and human suffering. Navigating the emotional aftermath of her divorce, Christine McVie poured her heart into her songwriting to create some of the most moving and long-lasting album tracks. A soulful confession of her then-secret romance with the band's lighting director, "You Make Loving Fun," caught the mixed pleasure and the natural complexity of love discovered outside of marriage. With its message of hope resonating with millions, "Don't Stop," an upbeat anthem about moving ahead and embracing the future, became one of the band's defining songs. And "Songbird," a gentle ballad highlighting McVie's sensitivity and her skill for creating ageless melodies, became a treasured classic with its message of love and resiliency spanning the decades.

The recording technique presented several difficulties. Tension and strife arising from the band members' personal problems sometimes permeated the studio. But this emotional intensity also inspired their inventiveness, driving them to probe hitherto unexplored areas of expression. Buckingham became a major player as his creative production methods and exacting attention to detail shaped the sound of the record. Working closely with McVie, he polished her tunes and helped her realise her musical vision.

With their unvarnished honesty and reflective lyrics, rumours became a cultural phenomenon, grabbing the hearts and brains of millions. Driven by band internal conflicts and sexual entanglements, the album topped charts all across and produced a run of smash songs. Rising to the Top 5 and thereby confirming McVie's reputation as a hitmaker, "Don't Stop" became an anthem of hope. Her moving ballad "Songbird," with Buckingham's subdued acoustic guitar accompaniment and her exquisite piano playing, demonstrated even more her talent to create songs that really connected with audiences.

Rumours drove Fleetwood Mac to unprecedented glory, but the personal cost was great. Christine and John McVie's marriage had split by the end of the tour, adding still another level of complexity to the band's already convoluted connections.

Despite personal conflict, McVie continued to contribute her songs and vocals to Fleetwood Mac's subsequent recordings. She co-wrote the Top 5 smash "Hold Me" from the 1982 album Mirage, and her song "Think About Me" from the 1979 double album Tusk, which peaked in the US Top 20. Her turbulent relationship with Beach Boys drummer Dennis Wilson inspired "Hold Me," therefore giving the song's poignant lyrics a personal resonance.

The release of her second solo album, "Christine McVie," in 1984 marked a significant turning point in Christine McVie's remarkable career. For the esteemed singer-songwriter, her self-titled effort—her first solo flight since her 1970 debut under her maiden name—marked a major shift. It was a statement of freedom, evidence of her artistic development and capacity to shine outside Fleetwood Mac's glittering galaxy. "Christine McVie," a captivating blend of pop sensibility, soulful vocals, and deeply personal lyrics, achieved both critical and financial success, solidifying McVie's standing as a formidable musical force.

The early months of 1983 marked the beginning of this solitary effort. McVie had a longing to more thoroughly explore her own creative terrain even as Fleetwood Mac rode the wave of success around their "Mirage" album. Though she had experience helping Robbie Patton produce his solo album, she knew she needed direction and turned to seasoned producer Russ Titelman, whose remarkable record includes work with Steve Winwood and Paul Simon. But Titelman's dedication to Simon's "Hearts and Bones" album pushed the McVie solo project's recording sessions to June 1983, allowing expectation to grow and creative ideas to stew.

The recording of the album turned Montreux, Switzerland, into a creative centre. Nestled among stunning surroundings and steeped in musical history, Montreux offered McVie the ideal setting for her to explore her craft. Over three months, McVie had a cooperative journey with a gifted group of musicians, each lending their special touch to her sound tapestry.

One particularly remarkable partnership was with Steve Winwood, a musical genius whose passionate vocals and piano mastery had graced venues and recording facilities all across the world. Initially, Winwood collaborated with McVie on Fleetwood Mac's experimental "Tusk" album and contributed his expertise to the song "Ask Anybody." Written years ago, McVie's song detailed her turbulent relationship with Beach Boys drummer Dennis Wilson. Winwood's natural grasp of McVie's vision shaped the song's arrangement; his trademark keyboard textures and soulful backup vocals gave McVie's emotional lyrics complexity and depth.

The surprising partnership with guitar great Eric Clapton was another record highlight. A longtime fan of Clapton's bluesy prowess, McVie invited him to help with "The Challenge," a song she said spoke to "life, regret, and rejection." With his trademark mix of soulful restraint and blazing intensity, Clapton performed a stinging guitar solo ideal for McVie's reflective words and catchy composition.

Other well-known musicians also helped the album, including Lindsey Buckingham, who supplied his unique guitar work and backing vocals to a few songs, and Mick Fleetwood, whose explosive drumming drove several tracks. Buckingham's inclusion on the record highlighted the continuous creative link between the two Fleetwood Mac members—even while they pursued separate artistic directions.

Audiences and critics alike connected with "Christine McVie," which also achieved both financial success and critical praise. Its peak of number 26 on the Billboard 200 list shows McVie's broad appeal and the album's accessibility. Two singles, "Got a Hold on Me" and "Love Will Show Us How," rose the charts and reached the Top 40, confirming McVie's reputation as a solo artist capable of creating appealing, commercially successful music.

McVie stayed a key component of Fleetwood Mac throughout the 1980s and early 1990s, helping them to keep on with albums like Tango in the Night (1987) and Behind the Mask (1990). Her Tango in the Night songs "Little Lies" and "Everywhere" became worldwide hits, therefore confirming her reputation as among the most consistent and successful songwriters in the band.

However, McVie ultimately suffered from the relentless pace of touring and recording. Her father died in 1990 during the Behind the Mask tour. This loss, along with her developing dislike of flying, led her to rethink her priorities. She kept helping Fleetwood Mac's albums,

Time (1995) and The Dance (1997), but her heart was no longer totally in the band's rigorous way of life.

Following over three decades of performing with Fleetwood Mac, McVie made the challenging choice to leave the group in 1998. Seeking a more sedate life free from the demands of celebrity and the emotional rollercoaster that accompanied being a member of one of the most popular bands, she withdrew to her English house. Although McVie's contributions to Fleetwood Mac's legacy would forever be evident in music history, this marked the end of an era for the band.

Later on, 2004 saw the release of "In the Meantime," the third and final solo album from Fleetwood Mac's songbird, Christine McVie. This introspective and deeply personal record marked a departure for McVie, not just from her band's collaborative embrace but also from the polished pop sounds of her previous solo efforts. Recorded in the tranquil sanctuary of her converted barn studio, "In the Meantime" offered a glimpse into McVie's reflective retreat from the limelight, a period of quiet contemplation and artistic exploration.

Following her departure from Fleetwood Mac in 1998, McVie sought a quieter life away from the pressures of fame and the relentless demands of the music industry. She retreated to her countryside home in Kent,

England, embracing a more reclusive existence. This tranquil setting, amidst the rolling hills and serene landscapes, sowed the seeds of "In the Meantime". The album's creation was a deeply personal and collaborative affair, with McVie's nephew, Dan Perfect, playing a pivotal role. Their musical partnership blossomed organically, beginning with a simple request for Perfect to add guitar to a demo titled "You Are." This initial collaboration sparked a creative synergy, leading to a series of songwriting sessions and the eventual decision to craft a full album.

The converted barn at the end of McVie's garden became their creative sanctuary, a space where they could experiment and explore without the pressures of external expectations. This intimate setting fostered a sense of freedom and allowed McVie to delve into her emotions with a raw honesty that permeates the album.

"In the Meantime" is a deeply personal reflection on love, loss, and the passage of time. McVie's lyrics, often introspective and melancholic, explore the complexities of relationships and the challenges of navigating life's journey. The album's title itself speaks to a sense of introspection, a pause in the relentless forward motion of life, a moment to reflect and take stock.

The album's musical landscape is as nuanced and introspective as its lyrics. McVie's signature piano playing, often characterised by its elegance and melodic grace, provides the foundation for many of the tracks. Perfect's guitar work adds a layer of texture and depth, ranging from delicate acoustic passages to more driving electric riffs. The album also features contributions from other musicians, including former Fleetwood Mac guitarist Billy Burnette, songwriter Robbie Patton, and McVie's ex-husband Eddy Quintela, each adding their unique touch to the album's sonic tapestry.

Despite its introspective nature, "In the Meantime" is not without its moments of raw emotion and even anger. Songs like "Liar" and "Bad Journey" reveal a darker side to McVie's songwriting, exploring themes of betrayal and disappointment with a raw honesty that is both compelling and cathartic. These tracks, inspired in part by McVie's exploration of contemporary music like Garbage's 1995 self-titled album, showcase her willingness to experiment with new sounds and push her creative boundaries.

While "In the Meantime" did not achieve the commercial success of McVie's previous solo efforts or her work with Fleetwood Mac, it remains a significant album in her discography. It is a testament to her enduring talent, her willingness to explore new creative avenues, and her ability to connect with listeners on a deeply personal level. The album's reflective tone and introspective lyrics offer a glimpse into McVie's inner world, revealing a depth of emotion and a vulnerability that is both captivating and inspiring.

In the years following its release, McVie expressed mixed feelings about "In the Meantime." She acknowledged its strengths but also admitted to feeling that she had "gone about it all wrong," citing her reluctance to tour and promote the album as a contributing factor to its limited success. Despite these reservations, the album remains a cherished gem for many fans, a testament to McVie's artistry and her enduring legacy as a songwriter and vocalist.

The recent reissue of "In the Meantime," remixed by Dan Perfect and featuring a previously unreleased track, offers a fresh perspective on this introspective and deeply personal album. It serves as a reminder of McVie's enduring talent and her ability to create music that resonates with emotional honesty and timeless beauty.

A TRIUMPHANT RETURN

Following years of calm retirement in the English countryside, Christine McVie found it impossible to resist the appeal of music and her lifelong friendship with her Fleetwood Mac colleagues. She first publicly performed in fifteen years in 2013 when she unexpectedly showed up in Maui, Hawaii, with the Mick Fleetwood Blues Band. Strong acclaim greeted this timid return to the spotlight, indicating that her musical enchantment had not lost appeal.

Later that year, McVie made a more significant move by joining Fleetwood Mac for two legendary evenings at London's O2 Arena. As she emerged, the audience erupted in cheers, as her presence invigorated the scene. She sang "Don't Stop," the hymn of hope she had co-written years before, reminding everyone of her ongoing influence on the band's legacy with her friends.

McVie's official return to Fleetwood Mac in 2014 came about thanks to this historic reunion. Fans from all over the world rejoiced after Mick Fleetwood made a statement during a concert in Maui. The band started a new chapter, their creative synergy rekindled with McVie back in the fold.

A unique creative collaboration emerged between McVie and Lindsey Buckingham, even as they utilised the full band dynamic. With their songwriting chemistry as strong as ever, they began working on new songs. This cooperation resulted in the 2017 joint studio album Lindsey Buckingham Christine McVie, which highlighted their combined skills.

Complementing the single "In My World," the album was a critical and financial triumph with a Top 10 in the US and the UK. It combined Buckingham's sophisticated guitar work and experimental edge with McVie's trademark warmth and melodic sensibility. To promote the album, the pair started a 38-date tour featuring Buckingham's solo work and songs from their joint endeavour among venerable Fleetwood Mac hits. For McVie, this was a rebirth that confirmed her creative energy was still as vivid as it had been. Her stage appearance exuded happiness and thankfulness, as she welcomed the chance to interact with people once more. Her return to Fleetwood Mac gave the band fresh vitality and reminded everyone of their ongoing impact.

However, when Lindsey Buckingham abruptly left Fleetwood Mac in 2018, the band experienced yet another transformation. To cover the void, Mick Fleetwood brought in Neil Finn, the Crowded House leader, and Mike Campbell, ex of Tom Petty and the

Heartbreakers. Although this new band kept touring and performing, many fans felt that Buckingham's unique guitar style and compositional contributions were missing.

McVie stayed dedicated to Fleetwood Mac despite this turbulence. Her passion for music and her relationship with her bandmates never wavered. In 2019, a BBC documentary, Fleetwood Mac's Songbird—Christine McVie, examined her life and career, highlighting her significant contributions to the band's success.

Released in 2022, Songbird (A Solo Collection) honours McVie's solo work and highlights her artistic flexibility. This library acted as a reminder of her songwriting and performance ability, both inside Fleetwood Mac and as a solo artist.

Christine McVie's path with Fleetwood Mac was evidence of her tenacity, creative energy, and lifetime passion for music. She made a lasting impression on the band's heritage from her early years as a fan to her indispensable roles as a vocalist, keyboardist, and songwriter. Millions of people were happy to see her back in 2014, which also confirmed her reputation as among the most adored and revered icons in music history. Although her time with us was brief, her music continues to inspire and uplift us, ensuring her legacy endures for future generations.

BEYOND FLEETWOOD MAC

Despite the close connection between Christine McVie's musical legacy and Fleetwood Mac, her creative energy surpasses band boundaShe provided her distinctive vocals to other musicians, thereby adding her unique touch to their musical landscapes. ouch. She joined Christopher Cross in 1988 on his song "Never Stop Believing" from his album Back of My Mind. Her voice fit his soft vocals. She also worked with former Fleetwood Mac guitarist Bob Welch on his solo "Sentimental Lady," therefore highlighting their ongoing musical relationship.

Like her music, McVie's personal life was full of happiness and sorrow. She married John McVie in 1968 under Peter Green's best man cover. Before starting separate tours with their individual bands, they celebrated with fellow musician Joe Cocker in a hotel in Birmingham rather than a conventional honeymoon. Their marriage had to negotiate both personal and professional demands in line with Fleetwood Mac's ascent to prominence. Their artistic connection transcended their personal disagreements, even after they divorced in 1976; they stayed friends and kept a close working relationship.

McVie took comfort in a relationship with the band's lighting director, Curry Grant, during the turbulent time around the rumours' recording. Though brief, this encounter motivated her to create "You Make Loving Fun," a frank and passionate statement of love and desire. She was romantically involved with Beach Boys drummer Dennis Wilson from 1979 until 1982, which served to inspire her creatively even more.

McVie married Portuguese pianist and songwriter Eddy Quintela in 1986. Their mutual love of music resulted in several joint projects, including the hit song "Little Lies." However, their marriage finally ended in divorce in 2003. Quintela departed regretfully in 2020.

McVie lived in Los Angeles and embraced the active California way of life throughout Fleetwood Mac's best years in the 1970s. However, in 1990, McVie sought a change of scenery and returned to England, purchasing a Grade II-listed Tudor manor home in the picturesque Kent village of Wickhambreaux, near Canterbury. Her haven became this old house, where she could re-establish her English roots and escape the pressures of celebrity.

The mansion gave McVie personal comfort and creative inspiration. She delighted in maintaining the ancient nature of the land and worked for years to restore it.

The peaceful countryside backdrop inspired her songwriting, allowing her to tap into a deeper reservoir of feelings and memories. She started spending more time in London after rejoining Fleetwood Mac in 2014, finally listing the manor property in 2015.

The music community grieved Christine McVie's death on November 30, 2022. She died after a brief illness at 79. It was then revealed that she had suffered a stroke and had been battling metastatic cancer with an unclear primary cause. Her loss left a hole in the hearts of her friends, supporters, and fellow musicians.

In a moving declaration of their great sorrow, Fleetwood Mac said McVie is "the best musician anyone could have in their band and the best friend anyone could have in their life." Her friend and musical partner Stevie Nicks expressed her loss and said McVie was "the best friend in the whole world."

Christine McVie's legacy goes far beyond her artistic successes. Renowned for her warmth, humour, and sincere love of her work, she was a gentle spirit. Millions of people found solace, delight, and a soundtrack to life's many chapters in her music. Even though her voice is now quiet, her songs still ring true, ensuring that her soul will continue through the work she produced. Though the songbird might have fled, her tunes will always linger in our hearts.

Printed in Great Britain
by Amazon